WINDOWS OF COMFORT

(Two Organbooks)

Organbook II

by

Dan Locklair

ISBN 0-7935-8183-4

e. c. kerby ltd.

DISTRIBUTED BY

HAL•LEONARD®
CORPORATION

7777 W. BLUEMOUND RD. P.O. BOX 13819 MILWAUKEE, WI 53213

WINDOWS OF COMFORT
Two Organbooks
by

Dan Locklair (b.1949)

Louis Comfort Tiffany (1848-1933), the American painter, stained-glass artist and glass manufacturer, created ten windows for the First Presbyterian Church of Topeka, Kansas, and they were installed in 1911. The windows are made of Favrile glass, a unique type of glass developed by Tiffany at his Tiffany Studios and Furnaces in New York. Not relying on paint for colour, Favrile glass instills its vibrant and jewelled colour palette directly into the glass itself. Viewed up close, the windows appear to be a kaleidoscopic array of colourful, precious stones. The secret to Tiffany's highly guarded, secret process for creating Favrile glass has never been divulged.

In the teaching spirit of the earliest Christian cathedral and church windows, the Tiffany windows of First Presbyterian Church use Biblical stories as their subjects. Except for the two Medallion Windows (where Trinitarian words and symbols are present), related scripture appears on each window.

In the pieces that make up the two organbooks of **WINDOWS OF COMFORT**, Mr. Tiffany's windows and their Bible texts have served as extra-musical stimuli. The stimuli for each piece came from a variety of dimensions, ranging from the impact of the smallest detail to the sheer drama of the complete window itself. Although each of the two organbooks is tightly knit within itself to allow each one to be played as a five-movement suite, it is also my intention that pieces from each organbook may be excerpted and grouped as the performer sees fit for recital or service of worship.

I wish to express my gratitude to all of the members of Topeka's First Presbyterian Church for their desire to celebrate, through this commission of music, their extraordinary Tiffany windows. Dr. Marie Rubis Bauer (First Presbyterian's organist) and Dr. Neil Weatherhogg (First Presbyterian's pastor) merit high and warm praise for their vision and resolve that has brought about the creation of **WINDOWS OF COMFORT**. Since I had the opportunity to view these windows prior to beginning work on this piece, I can attest to both their unique and stunning beauty as well as their Spiritual power.

SOLI DEO GLORIA!

To the performer:

Suggested registrations are given for a four-manual organ (the type found in Topeka's First Presbyterian Church). Manual indications are as follows: I = Choir; II = Great; III = Swell; IV = Solo (or Bombarde). The piece is conceived so that the performer may easily adapt **WINDOWS OF COMFORT** to either a two or three-manual instrument.

Organbook II

1. Matthew's Call
Window: ***The Call of Matthew*** (*"For I am not come to call the righteous, but sinners to repentance."* St. Matthew 9:13)
The melodic material on which this movement is based (D, F, E, F) comes from The Preces ("O Lord, open thou our lips.") that begins the Episcopal service of Daily Morning Prayer. These simple musical materials, along with transpositions and inversions of the idea, are put forth in dialogues of strength, boldness and persistence. The urgency of this "Call of Matthew" to "Follow Me" is as dramatic as is the sure reality of the challenges that The Call's acceptance entails. Here I have sought to express musically the dramatic and rigorous side of this test of faith.

2. "...a teacher come from God..."
Window: ***Christ and Nicodemus*** (*"Rabbi, we know Thou art a teacher come from God."* St. John 3:2)
The illuminating power of teaching is dramatically expressed in the third chapter of St. John's story of Nicodemus. The reflecting moon and always-illuminated lantern that are a part of this window seem to be symbolic of that power. Perhaps no hymn or psalm tune is heard earlier in childhood and more aptly reflects the Christian Church than does Bourgeois' Old Hundredth psalm tune from the Genevan Psalter set to the words "Praise God from whom all blessings flow...". As teaching transforms, so too has this well-known tune been transformed in this movement.

3. Bless the Child
Window: ***Christ Blessing Little Children*** (*"For of such is the Kingdom of Heaven."* St. Matthew 19:14)
The only piece in either organbook for manuals alone, **Bless the Child** is playful in a spritely, as well as somewhat unpredictable, manner. At the heart of the piece is the children's Pentatonic church school song, "Jesus Loves Me".

4. "...and call her blessed..."
Window: ***Christ and the Valiant Woman*** (*"God is Love, and he that dwelleth in love dwelleth in God and God in him."* I John 4:16)
In this window, the Woman represents the highest form of Godly love, reflecting both Proverbs 31:28 (*"Her children arise up, and call her blessed;..."*) and the window's I John inscription. Conceived for the warm foundation stops of the organ and supported by a rich harmonic backdrop, the continuous circular melody of this movement symbolizes the eternal truth that "God is Love".

5. Christ's Ascension
Window: ***The Ascension*** (*"And He led them out as far as to Bethany, and He lifted up His hands, and blessed them. And it came to pass, while He blessed them, He was parted from them, and carried up into heaven."* St. Luke 24:50-51)
This vibrant toccata celebrates one of the most radiant and uplifting events of The Bible. Like Movement 1, this finale is rooted on "D" (here, primarily Dorian mode). Also like Movement 1, rhythmical dialogue between the manuals is heard throughout the piece. Here a broader mid-section brings back the four-note Preces idea that was the basis of Movement 1.

Organbook II timings: 1. ca. **3'30"**; 2. ca. **5'30"**; 3. ca. **2'**; 4. ca. **4'**; 5. ca. **3'30"**   Total duration: ca. 18'30"

Dan Locklair,
Winston-Salem, NC
Autumn, 1996

To obtain full-colour slides of the ten Tiffany windows which inspired **WINDOWS OF COMFORT**, write to:
First Presbyterian Church, 817 SW Harrison St., Topeka, KS 66612 USA or call (913) 233-9601

*Commissioned by the First Presbyterian Church, Topeka, Kansas
in celebration of ten windows by Louis Comfort Tiffany in the
First Presbyterian Church sanctuary and dedicated to its pastor, Dr. Neil Weatherhogg, 1996*

Windows of Comfort
Organbook II

Dan Locklair

Suggested registration:

I: Founds. 8' 4' 2', mix(s)., III to I
II: Founds. 8' 4' 2', mix(s).,Tpt. 8
III: Founds. 8' 4' 2', mix(s)
IV: Large reed(s)
Ped: Founds., reeds 16' 8', 4', mix(s).,
    I, II, III to ped.

1. Matthew's Call

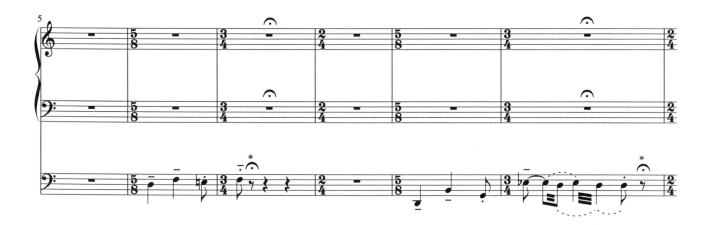

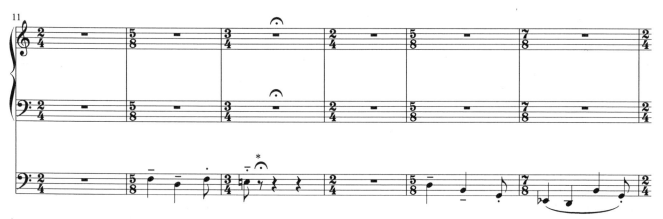

* In dry rooms, these fermatas should be very brief.
In reverberant rooms, the performer may wish to hold them longer.

4

* See note on previous page.

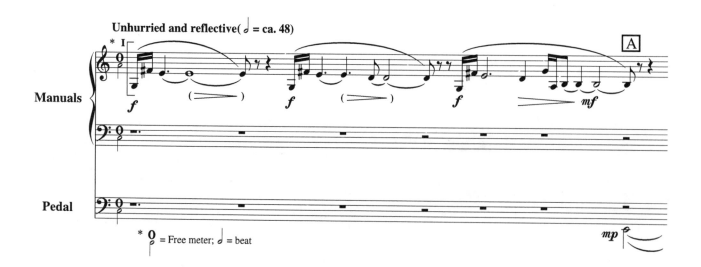

2. "...a teacher come from God..."

Suggested registration:
I: Solo reed 8' (opt. tremolo)
II: Diapason 8'
III: Flute (or string) celestes 8'
Ped: Soft 16', III to ped. 8'

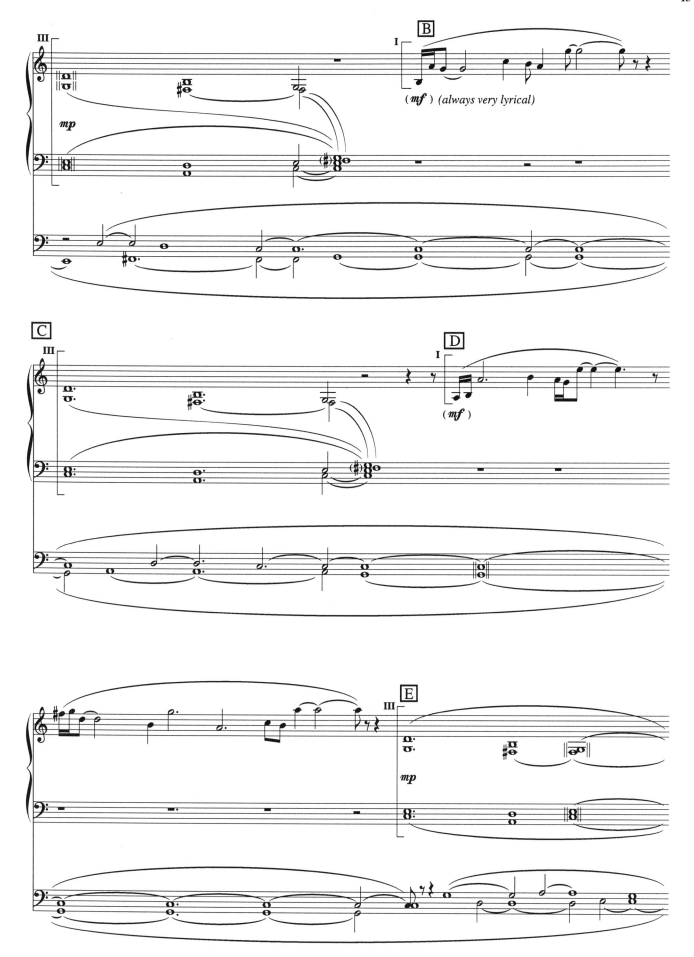

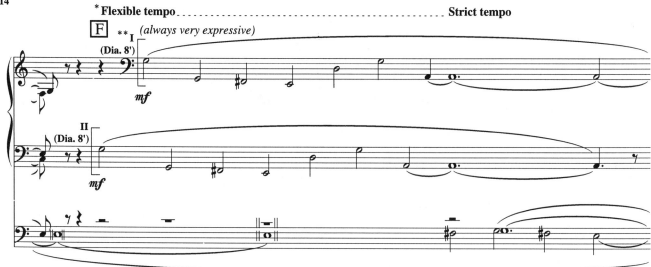

*Flexible tempo .... Strict tempo

F **I (always very expressive)
(Dia. 8')
mf

II
(Dia. 8')
mf

* One realization of this indication would be to move
the tempo forward toward the middle of each phrase,
then slow toward the end of the phrase.

** This second Diapason may be a bit softer than the L.H.,
but should always be audible as an echo to the L.H. sound.

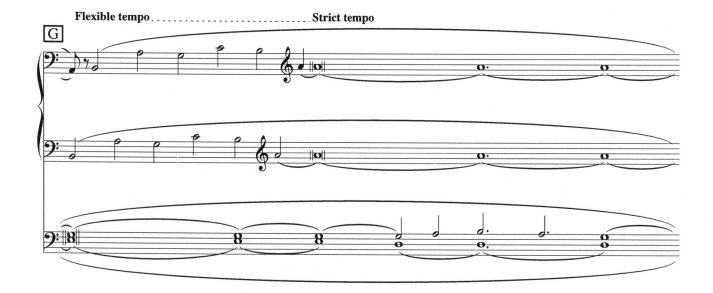

Flexible tempo .... Strict tempo

G

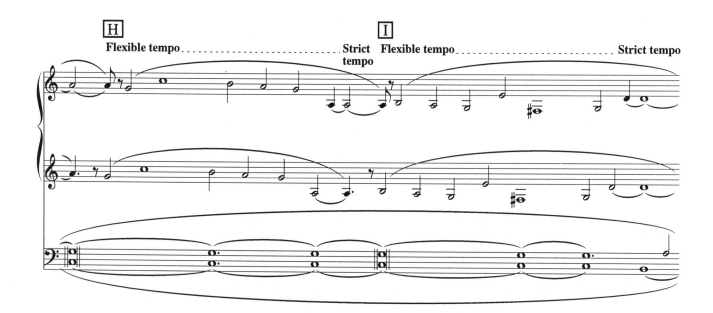

H Flexible tempo .... Strict
tempo

I Flexible tempo .... Strict tempo

Flexible tempo . . . .

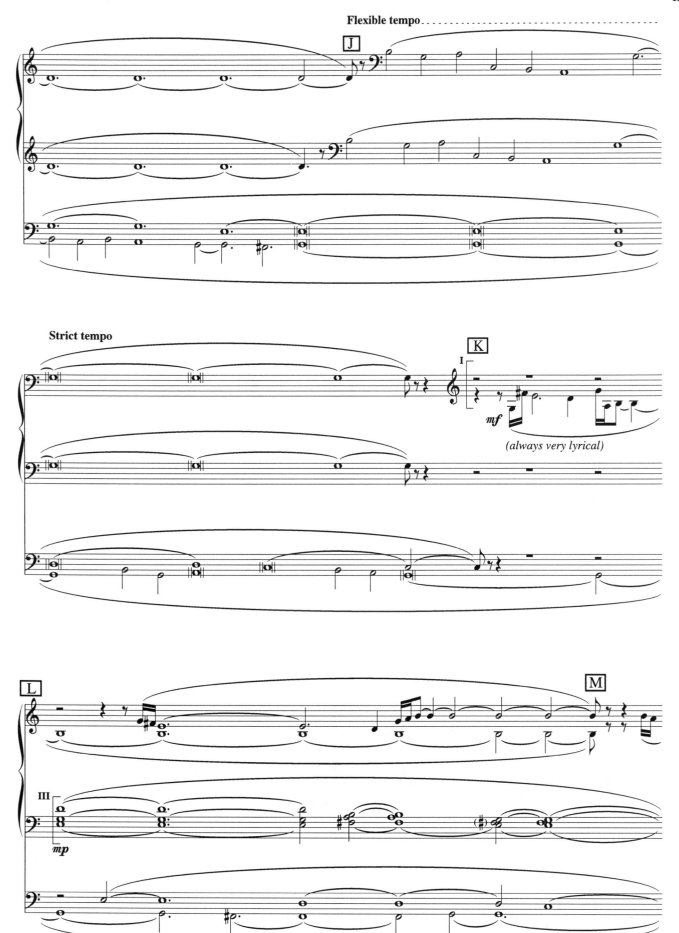

Strict tempo

(always very lyrical)

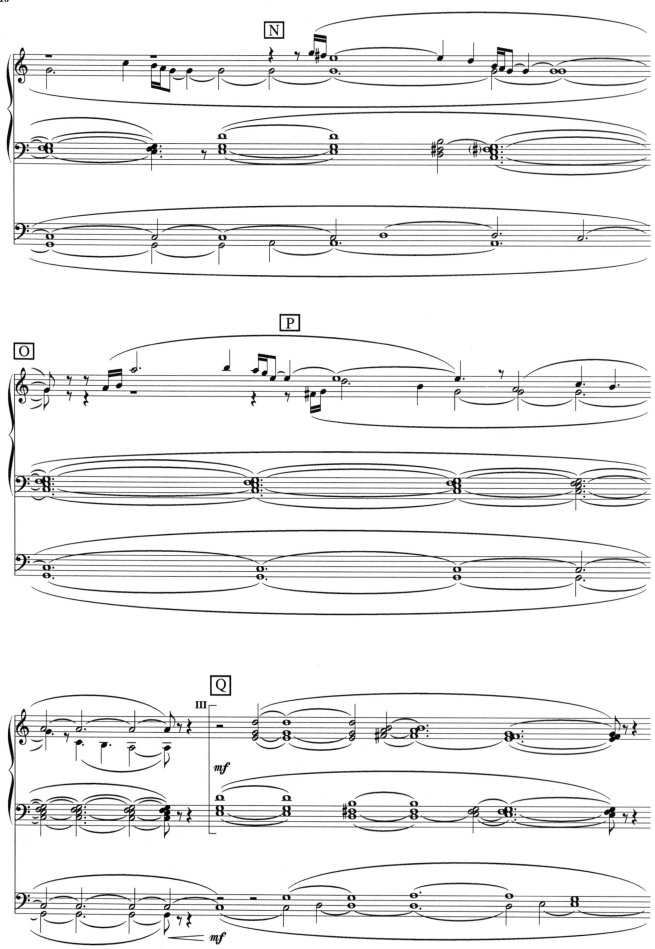

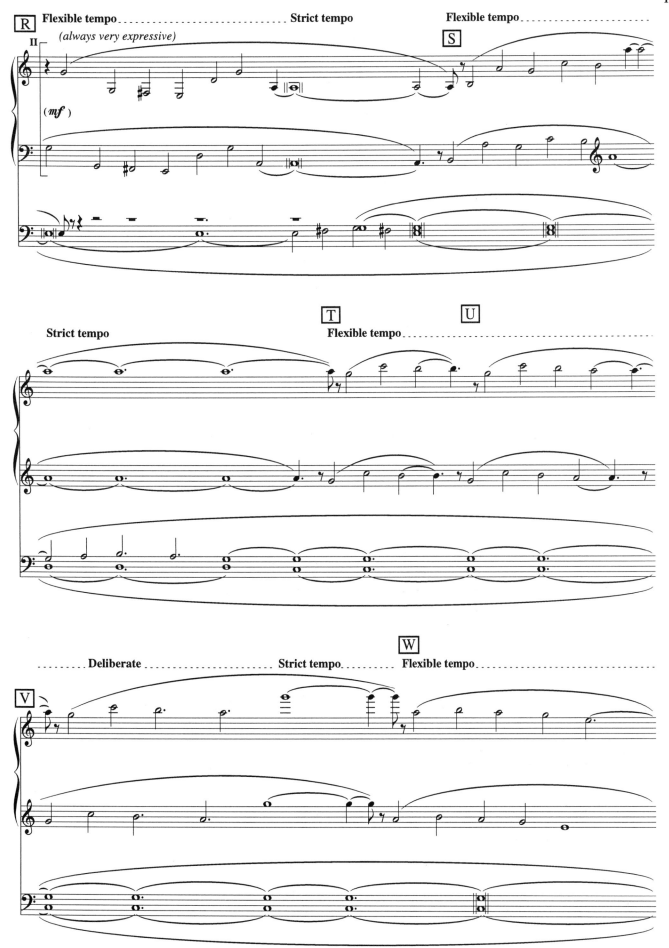

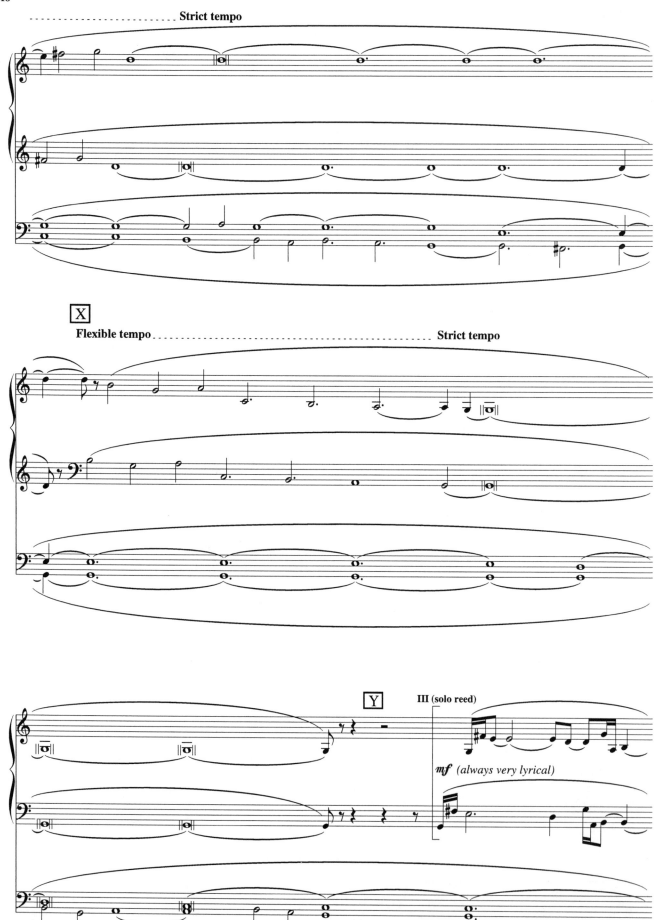

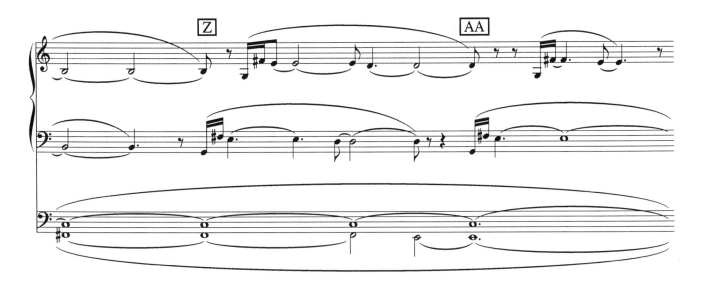

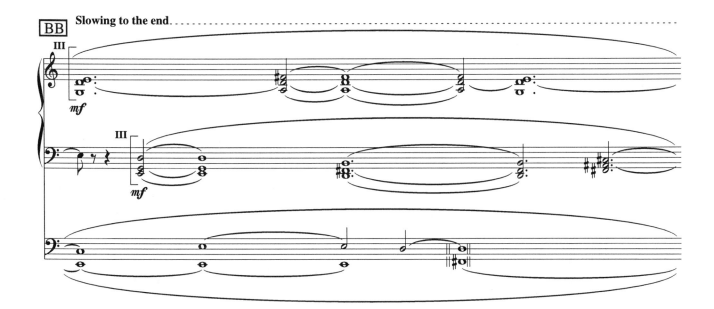

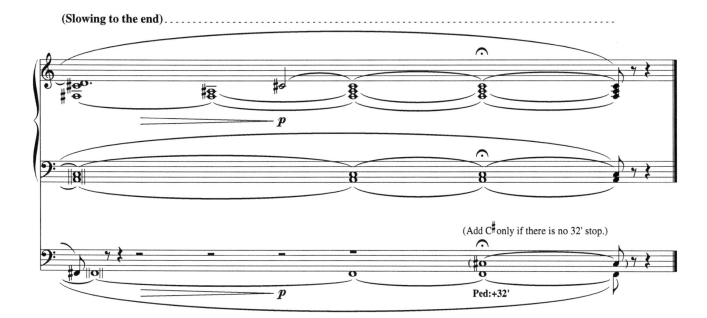

3. Bless the Child

Suggested registration:

I: Flute 8' (or Flute 4'), chimes
II: Flute 8', 2'
III: Flute 4'

* If there are no chimes (or harp),
  elongate each ("chime") note by almost double its length.

4. "...and call her blessed..."

*Suggested registration:
 I, II, III:
 Warm founds. and strings 8', 4'
 All manuals coupled to II.
 Ped. Founds. 16', 8', I, II, III to Ped.

*The entire piece may be performed on one manual (as marked) with no dynamic change,
or if desired, the performer may utilize manual changes to heighten the natural crescendo of the piece.

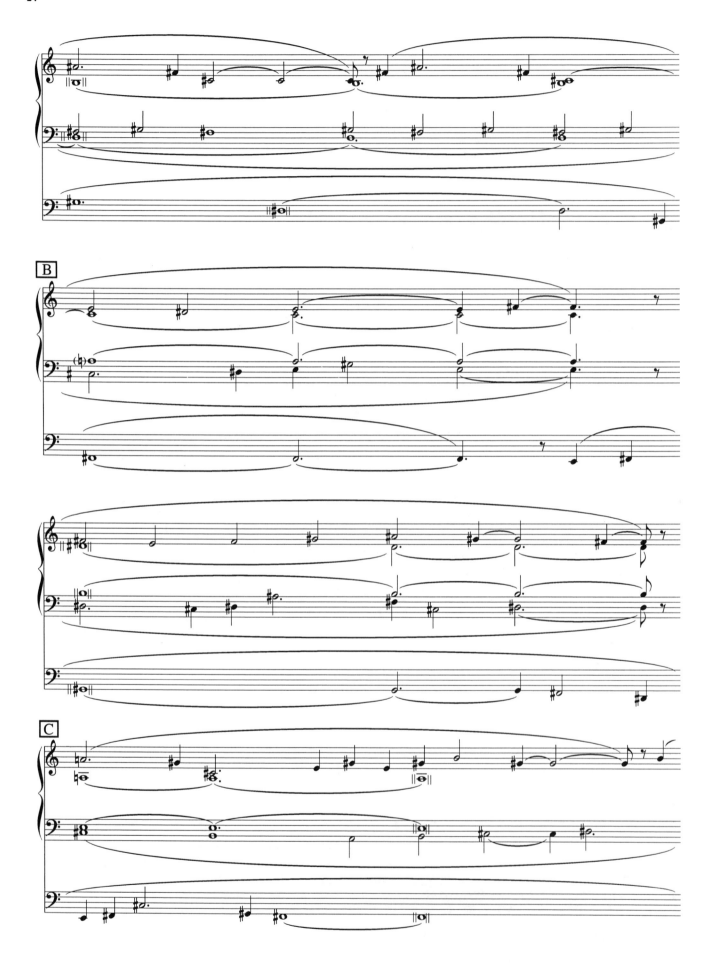

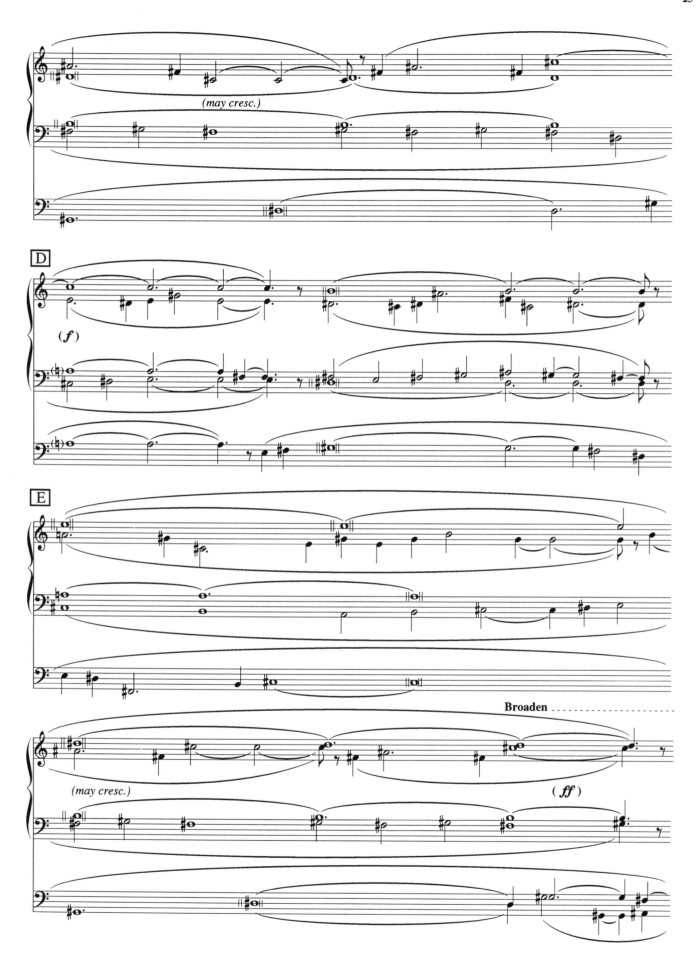

In tempo

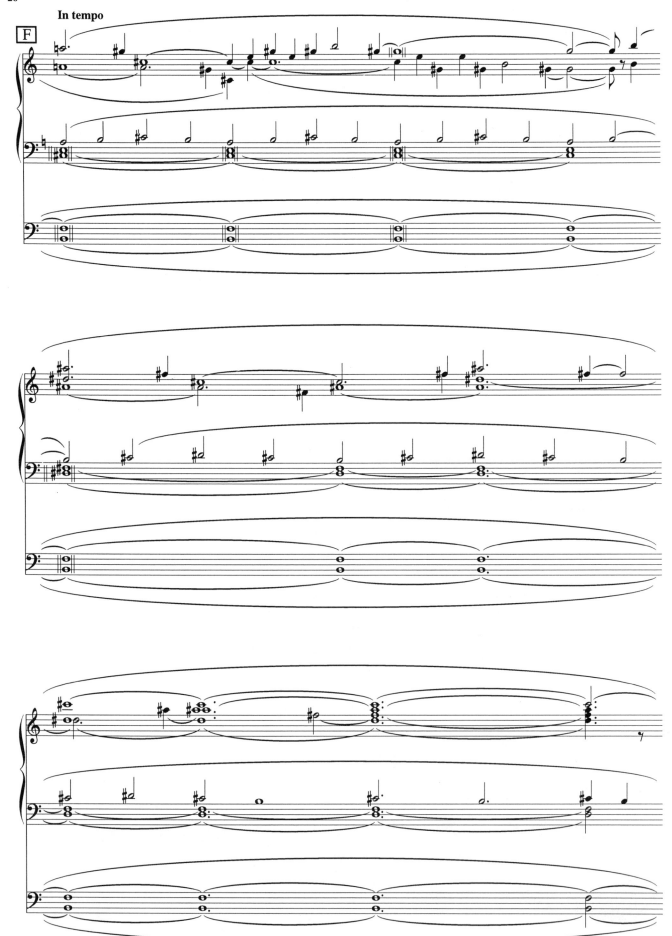

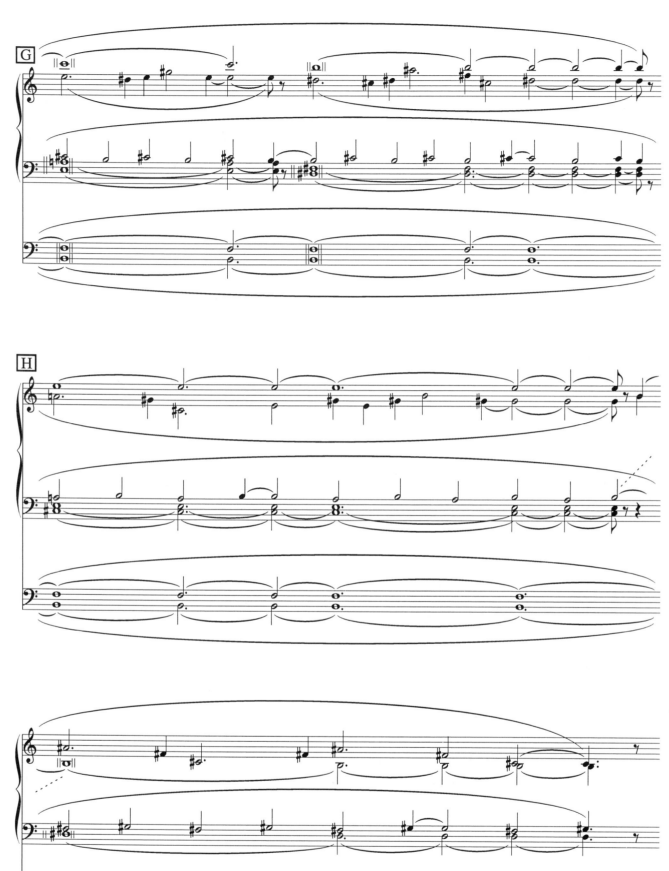

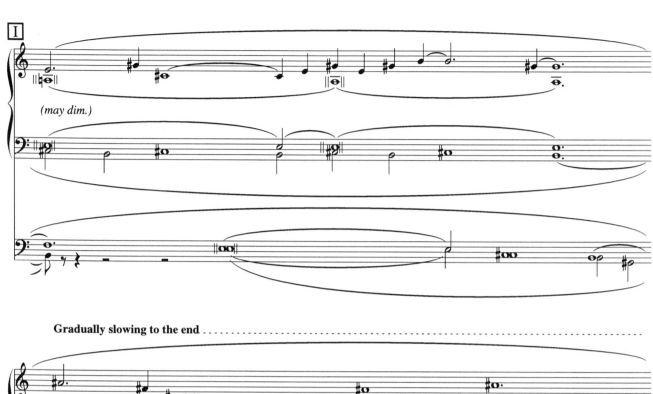

(may dim.)

Gradually slowing to the end . . . .

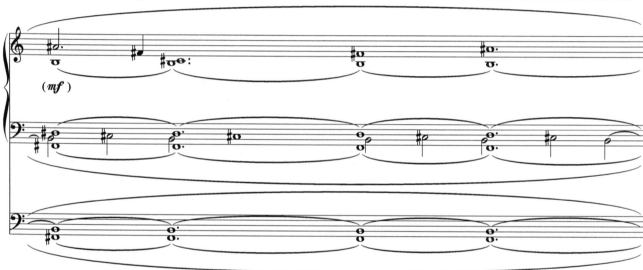

(mf)

(Gradually slowing to the end) . . . .

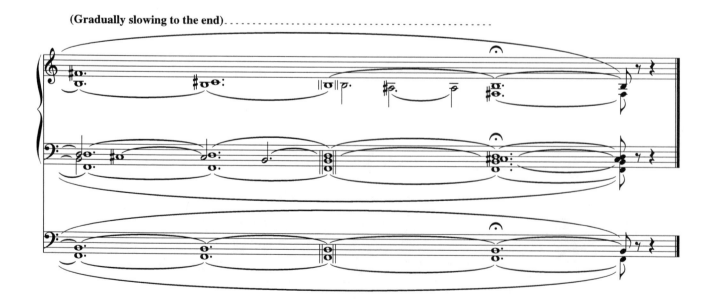

5. Christ's Ascension

Suggested registration:
I, II, III, IV:
Founds., reeds 16', 8', 4', 2', mixs.
All manuals coupled.
Ped. Founds., reeds (32'), 16', 8', 4', mixs.,
I, II, III to Ped.

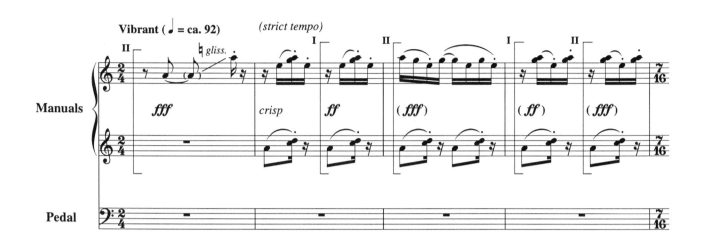

Manuals

Pedal

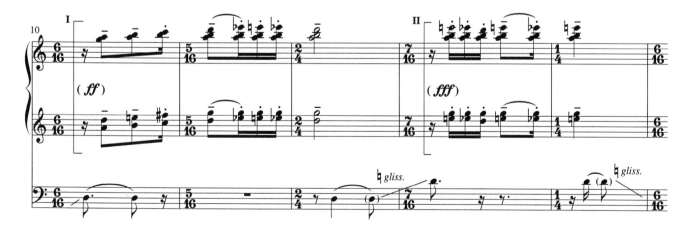

Summer, 1996
Winston-Salem, NC